What's Happening to My Child?

A Guide for Parents of Hair Pullers

ROPHE PRESS

Sacramento, California

©2005 Cheryn Salazar

Artwork created by Lyn Doiron

Dedication

This book is dedicated to my husband, Michael, who is the man of my dreams and my best friend. You have taught me so much. I truly thank God for you. Your unconditional love and support have made me the woman I am today.

To my incredibly wonderful children: Jessica, Alyson, Mikaela and Michael. You bring me more joy than I ever knew possible. I am truly blessed, and I love being your mom.

To Madison Noel Guthrie and Justin Campbell Guthrie, my precious grandchildren, and any future grandchildren! I absolutely love and adore you. You tickle my heart and bring me joy.

To Christina Pearson, who I appreciate and love from the depth of my heart. You are a gift from God, in so many ways.

To my dear friend and editor, Candy Chand, who has helped me tremendously to complete this book. Thank you for your marvelous editing (which makes me look a lot smarter than I am) and for all the support and encouragement you've given me along the way. You are absolutely fabulous!

And most importantly, I thank you, God, for all you've done for me, and for my family. Your love is evident in every aspect of our lives.

Table of Contents

A Message from Cheryn

Early in the process of creating this manuscript, the thought entered my mind that you, the reader, might wonder what qualifies me to write this book. The answer is, although I am not a doctor or therapist, I have struggled with Trichotillomania since the age of twelve, and I'm also the parent of four children, three of which have exhibited varying degrees of "Trich" behavior from a young age. Thankfully, they are all now, what I like to call, under management.

Over the years, I've discovered how to raise children who engage in healthy relationships, which include respect towards their parents, their siblings, and themselves, along with balance and moral awareness towards others outside the home. I believe much of this is lacking in the average home, though children raised in even the most functional households can still exhibit difficult behavior at times.

Today, I would describe my home as loving and highly functional, with much respect between our children, my husband and myself. Believe me, it wasn't always this way. Things just don't happen by magic. It's taken a great deal of hard work, applying information and effort through trials, along with grace and forgiveness, to develop the life we have today. My desire is to assist you with more than just help for your child, but to encourage you to grow in every aspect of your interpersonal relationships.

Over the years, while counseling parents of hair pullers, I've noticed a disturbing trend – desperate individuals trying to make their child stop by using mental, emotional and/or physical abuse. Understanding the feelings of the parent, I grasp the frustrating and overwhelming emotions they are often experiencing, and as a puller myself, I also know the devastating harm that inappropriate parenting can cause.

Unfortunately, in my case, there was no one to offer help when I needed it most. In fact, for the most part, serious aide has only been available since the early 1990's. My experiences with Trichotillomania were difficult, because I believed I was the only one who engaged in hair pulling behavior. And when my children exhibited early signs of the same disorder, I experienced a multitude of reactions. I felt embarrassment, shame, failure, disappointment, and an overwhelming dose of fear.

Until I was thirty years old, I kept my Trichotillomania a deep guarded secret. Up until that time, I had never met anyone with this condition, even though I learned in 1985, while in my early 20's from an Ann Landers article in the newspaper, that the condition existed. Consequently, I only told a few of my close friends about my hair pulling behavior, because I did not want to feel self-conscious or have them keep me at arms-length. I had become quite the pro at hiding my secret.

Eventually, I knew I had to tell my friends, because it was exhausting and crippling to constantly avoid exposure. Deep inside, I realized it was better to just tell them, even though I was terrified of rejection and criticism. When I finally began to share from my heart, much to my relief, the people who were loving and compassionate passed no judgment on me whatsoever, and the few acquaintances I told who responded in an inappropriate way made me realize quite quickly that I didn't want a friendship with them anyway.

One day, a friend of mine, Rene Strasser, was in a group setting where she heard Christina Pearson talk about her own hair pulling experience. After the others departed, Renee introduced herself to Christina, and told her a bit about me. The two women exchanged phone numbers, and the minute Renee got home, she called me. Excitedly, she chatted about her encounter with someone she believed was capable of relating to me on a deep, inner level. Immediately, I called Christina, thrilled to talk with someone who knew the depths of my pain, suffering, and isolation. Even though my husband and girlfriends were supportive, they still didn't understand me in the way I desperately needed.

Christina and I made plans to meet, but after several failed attempts over a two-week period, I had a pulling binge and called her in tears, my heart filled with despair and sorrow. She asked for my address, so she could mail me some information that she'd received from the Obsessive/Compulsive Foundation. It was then the situation turned miraculous.

I lived in a little community in the countryside of Santa Cruz, CA. So, as soon as I gave Christina my address, she let out a scream. Breathless, and in shock, she told me her home was only two houses away! I nearly fell over. It was late at night, and I was in my pajamas, but within seconds, we both ran out to meet each other in the middle of the road. Seeing her for the first time was like meeting my long, lost twin. She knew me like no one ever had. The entire experience was surreal.

Since that encounter, we've become close friends who have traveled extensively around the USA speaking at conferences and retreats for the Trichotillomania Learning Center, Inc. (TLC). Today my life has turned out far different, and more positive, than I would ever have imagined, because of the many blessings I've received by knowing someone as wonderful as Christina, working with

TLC, as well as from the lessons I've learned from actually having Trichotillomania!

I know some of this may be hard to believe. Growing up with such personal and deep struggles, even I never imagined my present life could be possible. And that, my friend, is why I'm writing this book. I want you to discover, as well, everything that's in store for you through the difficulties, or as they're sometimes called, "trials" you encounter. I truly believe trials are in our life for a reason. Gaining that outlook over time has opened my eyes to see the miracles and blessings rather than become bitter, cynical and immersed in self-pity. I've already had my share of negativity, so I speak as a person who feels she's a model after the Phoenix, a woman who's risen from her ashes.

I've said it many times before, and I'll continue to say it all my life—if I had a chance to relive my life again, and choose never to encounter this path of Trichotillomania, but not be who I am today, I would choose life with Trich. I don't say that lightly, for it's been a hellish road. For many years, I walked that path alone. I thought I might be emotionally unstable, having perceived such ideas from the critical looks, words and attitudes from people who just didn't understand. If you're a puller, I've felt your pain. And if you are a parent or a relative of a puller, I've also felt your pain.

As a child I didn't feel good inside my own

skin. I internalized my conflict and began to focus on my eyelashes and eyebrows as my problem instead of what was actually bothering me. I didn't possess the skills to be able to identify and thus deal appropriately with my emotions, so instead one day in seventh grade Social Studies class, I withdrew and separated myself from my external problems and emotions and began pulling out my eyelashes. Now I know there are many other scenarios that fellow pullers have in their experiences that are not founded on anything negative. Whatever the reasons your child began pulling, there is good news. The good news is that each of these reasons can be addressed which will benefit your child's overall well-being. My experiences, as well as those of many others, have shown that trials, or difficulties, are what mature us, create our character, and cause us to grow emotionally. Unfortunately, there are those who don't choose to work through their struggles and simply end up bitter and angry.

My deepest desire in writing this book is that it will equip you with the skills and knowledge you need to assist you and your child. I want to offer your child more than the freedom from pulling, but to help her* find a greater and deeper relationship with herself.

Since it is believed that more often it is the female, I will refer to the child in the feminine form throughout the rest of my book.

Yes, I believe, everything happens for a reason. I pray my struggles with Trichotillomania, both as an individual, and as a parent, will cast light into the depths of your darkness. May this book guide your family as you walk an often difficult and frustrating path. May you grasp, step by step, there is hope. But most of all, may you finally discover, you are not alone.

CHAPTER 1

WHAT IS TRICHOTILLOMANIA?

For many years, most physicians had never heard of the condition known simply as hair pulling, nor were they aware that a medical name had been coined over 100 years ago for the disorder by a French dermatologist named Hallepeau. There were, however, a few references in the Old Testament of the Bible that mentioned the syndrome. One is regarding Ezra who is documented pulling out his hair while in the deepest despair of the grieving process. Even Hippocrates, the father of modern medicine, spoke of the pulling of hairs as part of a diagnosis. And yet, doctors now seemed to have little or no knowledge of the problem!

Not until I was in my early 20's did I hear about another person with this condition, and it wasn't until my 30's that I actually met another individual, Christina Pearson, who had similar struggles. Christina is now the founder and Executive director of the Trichotillomania Learning Center in Santa Cruz, CA. Due to Christina's hard work, there is more information, and more research being conducted, to unveil the mysteries surrounding this complex disorder. Christina wrote up an easy-to-comprehend pamphlet years ago to help inform anyone interested in this disorder. She has allowed me to reprint a portion of her pamphlet in this chapter:

Trichotillomania is a disorder that manifests itself in the compulsive urge to pull one's hair, resulting in noticeable hair loss. Currently defined in medical literature as an impulse control disorder, the condition has come to light in recent years. This is the result of media attention on Obsessive-Compulsive Disorder. There are distinct differences in these conditions, but there is enough of an overlap that compulsive hair pulling is commonly included in what are called "Obsessive-Compulsive Spectrum Disorders." These include a variety of conditions that seem related to OCD, but do not meet actual OCD diagnostic criteria.

The term "Trichotillomania" is derived from the Greek words for hair (thrix), to pull out (tillein), and insanity, or frenzy (mania). It was coined in 1889 by a French dermatologist named Hallepeau for describing the case of a young man.

Trichotillomania affects an estimated 1.5% - 3.5% of our population, with approximately 80% of sufferers being female.

The Trichotillomania Learning Center (www.trich.org) has found that pulling has been reported in a child as young as four months old, and also found reports of pulling beginning late in life, after 70 years of age. But for most, there seem to be two types of Trichotillomania. The more benign form is often called "Baby Trich", and begins in children under 4 or 5 years of age, with many starting at 1 or 2 years old. There has not been a great deal of research, but it has been reported that approximately 50% or higher generally outgrow this "Baby Trich." But not all. So if a young child is pulling, you do need to pay attention, and act appropriately if necessary. For the majority of the more chronic pullers, the behavior usually appears in pre-puberty or at puberty, but it can emerge at any age.

The results might be as mild as one pulling ever so slightly as to not cause notice, while another might pull all their hair out from their scalp, face, and/or body. To help a non-puller understand, the act of pulling is actually very similar to any behavior that "self-medicates" or calms the nervous system such as nail biting or skin picking. The sensation from the actual pulling transmits an electrical nerve transmission that calms the pullers' nervous system. Another example you might be able to comprehend would be the anxiety a smoker, or addict of food or drugs experiences before having their "drug" of choice.

Trichotillomania is not well understood, and many different theories have arisen over why it exists. Once thought to be only a "bad habit", it is now described as a multi-faceted behavior. Since Trichotillomania has affected children as young as four months, it is concluded that the pulling of the hair is comforting, soothing, much like having your hair stroked. It is overall a "nurturing" type of activity to someone with the chemistry of Trichotillomania.

Anyone who feels overwhelmed to the point of needing to "shut down" and numb themselves, is a candidate for developing a behavior that will help "medicate" or distract them from their situation or anxieties. It's a dysfunctional way the body tries to take care of itself. Just as stress can settle in our shoulders, it can also manifest in other ways.

Feeling stress, from whatever source if overwhelming, can create in anyone the need to remove themselves from the uncomfortable emotions that surface, by creating a sort of box to climb into. That certainly is a sentiment shared by the majority of men, women and children I have spoken with regarding their own experiences and feelings. Our brains have been found to actually possess the predisposition of the manner it will take.

Often, but not always, a devastating circumstance will begin the cycle of pulling. Divorce, death, puberty, or perhaps a game of one pulling out an eyelash to make a wish, or seeing whose hair is the longest. Even worse than the devastation of having the experience of hair loss is the shame, embarrassment, hopelessness and depression that can impact so many aspects of the sufferer's life.

You must understand, there is help available! While this was not so much the case over a decade ago, it is more and more now. So please, be encouraged. I know many people personally, and have heard about many more, who have completely stopped pulling their hair, lashes, brows, etc. The good news is, many people today are bringing this condition under management.

Often people ask the question, "Is Trichotillomania hereditary?" Studies are still being made in hopes of discovering the answer to this question. However, so far, we know that some medicines, as well as Behavior Modification, (which help redirect the tension that often leads to pulling), have been helpful in reducing the desire to pull. The TLC Scientific Advisory Board is looking for medical answers and solutions, as they study the causes and effects of Trichotillomania. We are hopeful that someday Trichotillomania will be entirely eliminated. Many answers are on the way, however, funding is still greatly needed for research to continue.

TLC is continuing to offer support through their website www.trich.org, TLC's quarterly newsletters, retreats and conferences, nationwide support groups, as well as helping bring forth awareness through media attention. A wonderful documentary was made and recently released by TLC's president, Jennifer Raikes, called, "Bad Hair Life." TLC's goals are well stated in the organization's Mission Statement which is as follows: "Founded in 1991, the Trichotillomania Learning Center, Inc. is a nationally based nonprofit organization that works to improve the quality of life of children, adolescents and adults with trichotillomania (chronic hair pulling) and related body-focused repetitive disorders such as skin picking through information dissemination, education, outreach, alliance building, and support of research into the causes and treatment of these disorders."

Behavior Modification Techniques have been developed, and are often effective in helping those with Trich redirect the tension, as well as the habit, that often leads to pulling. Educated therapists and doctors, support groups, internet "Trich" chat groups, as well as my favorite which are the yearly retreats and conferences that TLC hosts, all offer the opportunity for helpful, applicable information and relational connection with others who share and understand the deep effects this disorder most often causes, especially to those that have believed they were the only one experiencing such pain. Each avenue is helpful in learning how to overcome the emotional and physical repercussions of Trichotillomania.

Quick Tips and Reminders

✦ Please remember, you are not alone. Did you know that up to 3% of the population exhibits some level of Trich behavior?

✦ Children as young as 4 months and as old as 70 years old have been known to exhibit some level of hair pulling behavior

✦ Trich.org is a helpful site with a multitude of informational and sharing passages for those who suffer with Trich, as well as for those who want to discover how to help someone overcome the difficulties associated with hair pulling.

❧ CHAPTER 2 ❧

IS THIS DESTINY?

Most likely what you believe about destiny will be determined by your philosophical or religious beliefs. As a Christian, I believe we were each created with a specific plan for our life, with trials on earth to help us grow and build our character. I know personally that the trials and lessons I've learned from Trich have certainly done that for me.

There are currently several genetic studies that are looking at potential heredity and predisposition factors, but there are no published results available at this time. Whatever the cause of Trich, I believe when a person is happy with herself, she won't have the need to turn outside for escape. I believe if we are raised to know our value, and truly feel our feelings, we won't be living anxiously and be compelled to numb ourselves with distractive behavior. That is why your role as a parent is so vital.

We now know that babies as young as four months old to adults in their 70's have been diagnosed with Trichotillomania. So, keeping that in mind, please realize, you are not to blame for your child having this condition. Trich is very similar to nail biting, skin picking, knuckle cracking, etc. It is the brains way to distract attention and/ or relieve anxiety. It is the same as if your child had attention deficit disorder, allergies, or a disease. No one is to blame. Trich is a condition that is tied to the nervous system. In a sense, it is the magnificence of the brain that causes this behavior, for our mind is capable of doing many things to relieve its own stress.

The reasons an individual might pull or act out an unusual behavior may range from curiosity or interest, or the behavior may derive from deeper issues. Since there are many reasons why someone might have developed Trich, and all cases are individual in nature, they need to be individually approached and addressed.

Why do any of us engage in behaviors that are destructive, when we really don't want to? I believe everyone exhibits some behavior in reaction to stress. I've yet to find anyone who doesn't utilize some method of distraction when they are anxious, depressed, etc. Whether it's to smoke, overeat, gamble, skin pick, crack their knuckles, or exhibit retail therapy, it still occurs. How much of our child's, or our own behaviors, are learned from our family dynamic and experiences? How was your relationship with your own parents?

I believe, we need to first examine ourselves as parents to help find the answers for our child. I'm a firm believer that children do live what they learn, and if we look within ourselves, we'll discover a huge pot of gold, answers to our own behavior and life problems as well. In a world today where there are so many disabilities in our youth, i.e. A.D.D, A.D.H.D, allergies, asthma, autism, to name a few, the question should be, "Why not my child?"

I believe, there are methods we can utilize to help decrease our child's anxieties so that her need to pull will be less prevalent. Sugar, caffeine, and lack of sleep are definite provokers of anxiety. I've found that if I ingest these ingredients, I am more prone to pull. However, as I improve my choices, my need to pull diminishes remarkably. These are the kinds of observances you need to make, so that you can help your child stay clear of unnecessary agitation. Many food disorders and negative behaviors derive from feelings of worthlessness and a sense of being out of control.

If your child is stressed, try to figure out why. Watch to see if your child is a perfectionist. (I used to think that was a positive attribute, but realized years ago, it wasn't. I re-taught myself to simply do my best, accepting that I'm simply not perfect. What a relief that brought me.)

I believe we have the most influence during our child's younger years, and that kids often mirror their parents' behavior. If your child is stressed, depressed, angry, etc. look at your own actions and attitudes towards her and see if you are perhaps contributing to her negativity.

How difficult it was, in the beginning, to look at myself and see the mistakes I made over the years. But, I believe, it's far better to look long and hard at ourselves, than to stick our heads in the ground, merely staying in denial. Our children deserve our best. Being a parent truly is a continual gift of sacrifice, but if we offer unconditional love from our hearts, the rewards will be eternal.

Quick Tips and Reminders

✦ Everyone deals with stress in his or her life in some behavioral fashion. Hair pulling is just one way the mind attempts to process stress.

✦ If you cut down on your child's intake of sugar and caffeine, and make sure she gets plenty of sleep, her anxiety level will likely be reduced. In many cases, this will, in turn, lessen her desire to pull.

✦ Watch for perfectionist tendencies in your child. Remember, no one is perfect. Try to encourage your child to accept mistakes as a testimony of her humanity.

♣ CHAPTER 3 ♣

IS THERE HOPE?

Yes, there is hope. Many people, both young and old, have stopped engaging in hair pulling behavior, although the status of their condition is probably more accurately referred to as under management, for it is an ongoing battle. Over time, the desire often lessens. I have experienced first hand freedom from the power Trich once had over me. I believe there is tremendous hope to overcome, but first, the person with Trich must do some inner work. This necessitates your child be engaged in a deeper relationship with herself, her emotions, and chemistry, so that she can learn to modify her life and behaviors, just as a person who has quit smoking or stopped any habitual behavior would have to do.

I still have occasional struggles with Trich, but the ability to overcome the hair pulling impulse has increased to the point where I'm now just left with the subtle habit. However, if I do ingest a great deal of sugar, or caffeine, or if I am over-tired, I will find my pulling desire increase and my resistance to the urges consequently decrease.

First, and most importantly, I've learned to accept who I am, continue to try to improve myself, and make right choices. I no longer experience shame, embarrassment, hopelessness and depression, but instead have a deeper understanding of myself emotionally and physically. I feel tremendous hope and happiness in my life.

Trich is no longer a dark cloud over my head. I'm free from its devastating grip.

Put the reality of Trich into perspective for yourself and your child. The disorder is not fatal. Instead, it's actually an indicator, or thermostat, that can reveal deeper issues. Over the years, I've spoken with many individuals who've had serious afflictions, such as an incurable disease or the loss of a limb, and I've been amazed at the depth of their maturity. They all held a special confidence and expressed a certain peace and joy, of which I felt deeply envious, and was determined to find for myself. Often, they spoke of their thankfulness for what their trials had taught them, and expressed they'd do it all over again, if they had the choice. That concept once astounded and intrigued me. Over the years, these brave and wise individuals have helped me put my struggles into perspective and to look at my trials in a new and enlightened way.

I began to ask myself questions such as: since everyone has struggles, could mine also serve the purpose of making me a better person as well? And, if they can be happy, can I possibly be happy, too? I knew instinctively that the answer was yes. It was as if, with their help, I'd put on an entirely new set of eyeglasses and began to see the world through a more positive perspective. That is what I'm hoping you can do as well. If you can, you will gain more than you might imagine. On the other hand, nothing but frustration will result if you choose not to. My desire is to infuse your heart with hope and to help you see the opportunity you have before you— to draw closer to your child, and your child to you, instead of allowing Trich to keep you apart.

Your position as a parent is a wonderful opportunity. Ultimately, you are intended to be a covering (protection) over your child. With your love and direction, she will have a better chance of knowing who she is and will someday be able to teach her children as well, positively impacting many generations to come. When a child sees her parents have confidence in her, instead of merely a critical eye, it helps her become emotionally healthy, and to have healthy tools to parent her own children in the future.

I want to encourage you by sharing that my two children with Trich have followed these methods and are no longer driven by their behavioral impulses. Their self-esteem is high and their need to pull is not the constant presence it used to be. As they've learned to address the issues and situations that often provoke the desire to pull, their compulsions have become less, and occurrences have become minimal.

In the process, our family has become closer since we've learned to interact fully with mutual respect and understanding. I've studied and inquired much since my children's toddler years about how to raise kids with emotional health and well being. This includes a healthy relationship with respect towards their parents, each other, and themselves, along with balance, moral awareness and respect towards those outside their home.

As I've spoken with many parents and grandparents of hair pullers over the years, I've found there was often abuse towards the individual with Trich, as the family members tried, in their own way, to "help" their loved one stop pulling. Most often this was done out of compassion, but laced with fear, which can influence the techniques chosen to try to "remove" this "bad" behavior.

I've been a mom for 24 years and have worked diligently with my own family to learn how to have healthy, functional relationships and to teach them to have the same towards themselves, their parents and each other. My oldest child, Jessica, began pulling at age 5, resulting in loss of eyelashes for many years. She is 24 now, and occasionally deals with Trich, but for the most part is under management. My other daughter, Alyson, has more the impulse than the behavior, and has been able to avoid pulling by applying behavior modification methods, which I will discuss later in this book.

My biggest fear used to be to have a child with Trichotillomania. When parents tell me of their pain, I remember how I felt when Jessica came out to the living room displaying her missing eyelashes. My heart sank. Fear shot through me and shame came over me. Embarrassment and emotions ran so deeply, it was hard to even look at her. Then I felt guilt for experiencing those feelings.

It would be years before I got help for myself, but out of my love for Jessica, I was determined to figure out how to help her. Nonetheless, I hardly knew where to begin. The only thing I was clear about was, I had to let her know that whenever she wanted to pull, night or day, she could come to me. Fortunately, she did, pretty faithfully. Knowing from my own experiences that she'd most likely be feeling anxious and stressed, I'd hold her in my arms, rub her back, head, feet and hands, and ask her what she felt was the reason she wanted to pull. Often she wouldn't know right away, but as began to relax in my arms, she'd try to express what she was feeling. "Kids weren't nice at school today" or "School work is stressful" were a few feelings that came tumbling out. I, in turn, would try to support her and diffuse the issues by putting her concerns into proper perspective. Eventually, she'd go back to her bed and to sleep, most often no longer tempted to pull. I realized the greatest gift I could instill in Jessica was her incredible preciousness and value. I made sure I didn't focus on myself, but instead on Jessica and her feelings.

Today, Jessica is 25 and a wonderful, healthy

adult. She occasionally struggles with pulling, but the temptation doesn't factor into her self- esteem. She just looks at the behavior as something she occasionally does, but not as an indication of who she actually is. I'd say, and most importantly she will say, that she has gleaned tremendously from her trials. I've heard her tell others, she too would choose to have Trich if she had the chance to live her life over again.

Two of my other children have also had some degrees and variations of Trich. Yet, they are all healthy and happy individuals who have learned to look at their trials through different glasses and recognize they are better off from the struggles they've experienced.

When Jessica began pulling I felt so many feelings. I felt fear for her future; I knew too well the taunts and ridicules from others and didn't want her to go through what I had experienced. I wondered if she would suffer like I had. I felt embarrassment that it might call attention to the fact my eyelashes were also missing. Would others notice I didn't have any eyelashes too and then blame me for her condition? I could hardly look into her eyes. I felt such guilt, failure, and disappointment.

In contrast, I remember feeling glad that at least I could relate to Jessica because of what she was feeling. I knew too clearly how lonely this road had been for me, still believing that I was the only one who did this "terrible and disgusting" habit. Jessica was actually the instrument in my life to start asking questions that I had never before felt prompted to ask. I could see her preciousness and value, regardless of whether she had facial hair or not. It helped me to think about myself that way, too. Her struggle with Trich began a healing in me as well, a healing of love and acceptance.

Having a child with Trichotillomania was actually the inspiration for me to begin this search for help; not just for her, but also for myself. I thought the least I could infuse into my daughter was that her value and preciousness was not and never would be determined by her appearance—a fact that many people still don't understand in our society today. I want you to understand that principle as well, so you will be able to draw closer to your child instead of pushing her away, and that you will be able to empathize with what your child is going through and be able to effectively help her.

Pulling met an unknown need at the time, but as I learned about what Trich was, and why I had it, I began to discover there were events that preceded each pulling episode, and if I were to tune in and identify those feelings, I could learn to diffuse the issues, which then lessened my need to pull. When I came to a point where my chemistry didn't aggravate my pulling as severely, the new discipline

I had developed over the years brought me to a place where I was also able to deny my impulses. That is when behavior modification helped me so much.

Help your child to find her voice, her authentic self. Believe me, this is a gift you can offer your child in this very confused society. Teach your child that magazines and the world's standard of self-worth is often warped. Youth, wealth, thinness, beauty are praised; the handicapped and elderly are discarded as less-than. Express to your child the value and the richness of finding her beauty from within. Those worldly values often keep a person living on the outside of who they are, keeping them from emotionally developing and maturing.

As we learn to identify our feelings, we can then appropriately handle them and the need to pull will lessen. It's much like the smoker who quits still needs to feel her feelings, walk through them, and handle issues rather than simply resorting to a cigarette. It takes time and much effort to make this happen. Some kids aren't ready until they've first learned to love themselves. Some are ready to address issues right away. It's all up to them and their individual timing.

I know in my life, certain things have taken years for me to accomplish. Cooking was difficult for many years. Then when I hit 40, I was finally freed up in the kitchen to experiment and have fun.

Things changed for me as I changed inside.

Your child will change too, when she is ready. It's up to you to gently guide and encourage her along the journey. Remember, your child is not too slow. Her timing is always perfect.

Quick Tips and Reminders

✦ Be a positive covering/influence over your child, encouraging her to see the life lessons wrapped inside her struggles.

✦ Be a safe place for your child to run. Allow her to open up and share what is causing her stress without fear of criticism or ridicule

✦ You can't rush progress. Your child's timing is always perfect. She'll be ready to initiate change, not when you tell her to, but when she knows the timing is truly right.

❧ CHAPTER 4 ☙

WHAT'S A PARENT NOT TO DO?

The first thing you shouldn't do is panic. Fear will only perpetuate negative reactions towards your child. Issues with shame are an enormous part of the pullers self-esteem and actually a strong precursor to pulling. It can create a vicious cycle when wrong actions are administered. You need to understand as a parent that this disorder is much bigger than anything you feel you could have done to cause it. Even if you have contributed to many of your child's stresses, you didn't cause your child to pull. It is a genetically disposed behavior that reacts to stress with the manifestation of pulling. Pulling is just how your child's brain tells her to relieve stress, boredom, or anxiety.

You need to stop blaming yourself for your child's condition. Disciplining, punishment, shaming, and/or trying to control your child is also not the answer. Let us look at what you might do to help her change her behavior and let's also look at what you might be doing that might add to her anxiety.

Your child needs you to surround her with a nurturing and loving environment within the home. But, remember, ultimately this is her battle to fight. As much as you want to help her stop, to make her stop, it just won't help. Let me say it again, it will not help. Such attempts will actually make things more difficult for her in the long run.

Around eight years ago, I wrote my first book, You Are Not Alone: Compulsive Hair Pulling—The Enemy Within. After sharing my Trichotillomania story, my heart has developed a new burden, regarding the abuse that parents often unknowingly cause their children. Some abuse has stemmed from deliberate shaming, punishment, etc. Other abuses have come from ignorance in understanding what Trichotillomania really is, and how it claims its victims. Many parents just don't grasp that their children don't wish to engage in this behavior.

After the release of that book, I received many calls from parents and grandparents of children with Trich. There was a familiar thread through many of their stories regarding some form of abuse they were inflicting on their child. Some were physically punishing the child to try to control and/ or discourage her from pulling. Some shamed their child, even ostracizing her from family outings, often due to their own embarrassment of their child's appearance. I've even heard of spiritual condemnation being put upon children, as parents told their kids they were sinning every time they pulled a strand of hair.

In response, I would share from my heart, over the phone, and at conferences with parents frustrated about what to do with or for their child. It was so wonderful, after most conversations, to see a light bulb go on and a sense of relief take over these parents, who were trying their best, but reaching out in the wrong way. I've seen many relationships change from being stressed and distant to being healed and close.

If you are a parent who demonstrates any of the characteristics I just spoke about, please go to your child and apologize, tell her your intentions were good, but you were mistaken about how to handle things properly. Tell your child you love her, and will continue to love her, whether she has hair or not. You can be to her what she can't yet be to herself. You are a covering over your child, that can protect her from the harmful darts of an often hurtful world.

I'm so thankful you're reading this book. I'm grateful you want to better understand Trich and your child. What a comfort your child must feel, even if she doesn't show it yet, to realize her parent is learning as much as possible to offer the help and support she so desperately needs. As a parent, you can help your child get a sense of mastery over her own life. For a child, to learn to be disciplined and rule over her emotions is a huge gift that will keep paying the rest of her life.

Today, I'm productive and at peace with myself, accepting the imperfections I long ago fought. I can honestly say that through all the trials, Trich has taught me priceless blessings and taken me through a path that has made me into a person with compassion and insight that I believe I would never have learned otherwise.

If you feel you have been hurtful to your child, don't let another minute pass without going to her and asking forgiveness for any mistakes you've made. Let her know your heart was never to wound her spirit. You simply wanted to help her but were overcome by frustration. Encourage your child that she is not the only one with this affliction, that many people have stopped pulling, and that you will do whatever you can to support her as you walk this journey together.

Quick Tips and Reminders

✦ Stay calm. Don't panic. Your child will follow your lead. Always react with a gentle spirit, knowing your positive attitude will rub off on your child.

✦ Stop blaming yourself. You did not cause your child's hair pulling behavior.

✦ If you've ever abused your child—spiritually, emotionally or physically—in an attempt to control her Trich, apologize today. It's not beneath good parents to admit they're wrong. Humility and forgiveness are part of the healing process.

CHAPTER 5

WHAT'S A PARENT TO DO?

My hope is you will be able to build a relationship with your child that is supportive, loving, and that will help your child grow into a healthy adult, confident that her value is assessed not by what she does, but simply by whom she is—a precious and valuable human being. I want your home to be a safe place and for you to be a safe person whom your child can trust.

By having your home become a safe environment for your child physically and emotionally, she will have a place of refuge in this often dangerous and hurtful world. When other kids tease her, she will be better equipped to cope, because she'll know she has a support system of people who love and accept her for who she is. Ultimately, she will choose better friends and not gravitate towards anyone who will have her. With your help, your child's choices will become more selective. A child that feels valuable and loved will not be drawn to people who engage in inappropriate behavior. Drugs will find no appeal to someone who doesn't want to shut down and feel numb. If her parent loves her in a healthy and unconditional way, she won't want to have anyone in her life that offers her less.

Any parent knows that in the best circumstances raising children can be a difficult and an overwhelming responsibility. Add a compulsive hair pulling condition to the mix and that can leave parents, as well as their child, feeling hopeless and unequipped to address and deal with the obstacles. Understanding that, you must first forgive yourself for the mistakes you've made. Then, ask your child to forgive you. Often in our attempt to guide our children in the way that we think is right, we cause hurt and alienation. Our intentions may be good, but our methods inappropriate. Let's face it; most of us were not raised in the healthiest of families, and therefore we simply live what we've learned.

Be sure to open up lines of communication. Ask for forgiveness for mistakes and communicate how you as a parent tried your best, but sometimes didn't know how to handle the struggle correctly. It's always a healing, and a sacred moment, when I confess my frailties to my children and ask for their forgiveness. It's helpful for children to know their parents are not perfect. It allows them the grace to forgive themselves and to acknowledge their own mistakes as well. While some parents believe admitting their wrongdoings might cause their children to lose respect for their authority, I believe the opposite is true.

Approach your child with compassion and empathy. All of us have a habit or two: nail biting, knuckle cracking, skin picking and overeating are a few of the ways we handle stress in our society. Although these methods are more acceptable, it's really all in our perception. Showing your child that she is not alone, that you love her unconditionally, and nurturing her development of a strong sense of self-esteem are the most important gifts you can give her.

When you take the time to learn about Trichotillomania, and gain insight to your child's suffering and what she experiences with Trich, it will draw the two of you undoubtedly closer. Many have shared with me how my first book, You are Not Alone, helped them understand their child's feelings and opened up a door of communication and a deeper relationship between parent and child. When parents invest time to read about something that will help their child's well-being, and to understand better what their child is experiencing in her trials, this will open a doorway for a deeper level of intimacy.

Another suggestion is attending a TLC conference together, or by yourself/herself, if your child is mature enough, which is put on annually by the Trichotillomania Learning Center (www. trich.org). Without a doubt, the more you know, the better equipped you will be. The retreats often result in better communication and bonding between parent and child. The TLC workshops for parents, as well as for children, are wonderful and present many professionals offering a wealth of information and aids. In addition, this will get your child together with other kids who share her sorrows and experiences. I promise you, this process brings forth healing, encouragement, and progress. One of the things I love so much about the annual TLC retreats is to watch the kids transform, and so quickly, too. The hope that they gain from being around others, realizing they are not alone, and the information they learn from workshops, gives them the strength they need to change their perception about themselves. They, as well as the parents, and all the other attendees, leave with a much different, and more positive, outlook than when they came. So, my hope is that you, too, will attend and end up with an entirely new vision regarding your child and her experiences.

It's as important for you to understand that your child is normal, as it is for your child to understand that about herself. Helping your child realize that everyone struggles with some difficulty in their life will help her feel better about the obstacles she is trying to overcome, and will help her maturing process regarding a multitude of life battles. You need to realize, and to also help your child to understand, there is a purpose in her having Trich. Without hope, your child will struggle with unnecessary inner doubts. If you were able to reach in as a parent and remove this disorder from her experience, you would be robbing your child of the life lessons she needs to learn through her struggles, trials and sufferings.

I believe many parents battle self-condemnation when their child has Trichotillomania. I know I went through similar emotions. Condemnation and blame bring forth a type of death. If you can let go of that lie, and see your child's condition accurately, you'll provide your child with a new perception as well. If you have hope and a vision, she can grab onto yours and learn to change her life. Kids truly do model their parents. The advantages of what they'll learn will far outweigh the difficulties they experience while getting there.

Trust that every struggle in your children's life, just as in your own, teaches valuable lessons. It is during those struggles that we grow. Think about it—Trich makes us grow! Trials teach us lessons and skills. Trials are cathartic; they are extremely purposeful, and act as teachers in our lives. So, don't resist trials. Instead, look for opportunities to grow. Recognize that this is your child's path. Trust the process. Let go.

Create an opportunity to teach your child about choices and perception. Examine and challenge the filter by which you view the world. Changing your perception of Trich will help your child change hers. When she can begin to see her value and worth, many of her anxieties will begin to melt away.

As the parent, you can help define or discover root issues that might have stirred anxieties in your child's emotional makeup. When I first began pulling, I was twelve years old. I had no one in my life that understood my feelings and experiences, let alone knew how to give my condition a name. The pain and suffering I went through was difficult, primarily because I felt so alone. Consequently, I began to love almost anyone who showed me acceptance. I still have deep fondness for a few friends' parents for this very reason.

However, I now realize that a bit of my emotions were on the side of being dysfunctional/ inappropriate. To make my point, recently, I contacted several people from my past by browsing an Internet telephone book. As I looked for one particular friend, I saw her mom's number and gave her a call. Much to my dismay, she showed very little interest in return. I realized, as I thought about our encounter, it really wasn't that there had ever been much between us, but it was that she had been kind and non-judgmental in my teen years when I needed it so very much. My point is, as parents we need to learn to be caregivers who accept our children and love them unconditionally. It doesn't mean we condone inappropriate behavior, or don't set rules, but that our kids know we are a tender place they can come home to.

When my oldest children entered their teens, my husband and I took a course on how to raise older kids. The first thing the class addressed was our own issues – giving us the opportunity to look at how we were raised. At first I thought that was odd, but then quickly it resonated that the way I parented was reflective of how my parents had parented me.

For myself and for my children, I needed to learn why I am the way I am— intense and anxious at times. Then, I began to ask myself, "When are those times? Why do I become anxious? Am I a stressful parent? Is my child actually reflecting my moods? Is appearance how I define my worth?" In answering my own questions, I discovered a great deal of fear within myself, not quite believing I was valuable and loved. When I began to re-parent the little girl inside of me, changes began to occur.

As I saw my own pain and hurts, and was able to work through them, I had a better foundation to be a better parent to my children. I encourage you to do the same, if needed, ideally with the help of a counselor, a class, or at least with the assistance of a good self help book.

You may not be able to understand how Trich behavior feels good to the puller, but respectfully understand that their chemistry is different then yours, so you won't react with criticism or shame towards your child. Why my brain tells my mind that my brow or lash is as big as a log, and has to be removed, I don't know how to express the drive I feel. It's like an unwanted chin hair; it's just gotta go! I believe my brain transfers my stress/anxiety onto the follicle, and it becomes my focus, temporarily removing my attention from the true issue at hand. It is definitely a coping mechanism.

I'm often amazed that if I can wait a few days, that huge unwelcome follicle mixes back into its landscape, and I forget about it—an almost impossible feat just a short time earlier. My brain sometimes baffles me. Trust me. It's a tough disorder/condition to deal with. When a person with TTM wants to pull, it feels like there is a spotlight on that hair, lash or brow. Nothing else matters but the need to remove that follicle. Sometimes even enough to dig for it! Many times, when I've pulled, I've done so without regard to the outcome. The drive is so strong I just want to complete the mission.

One might graze for hours, looking and searching for that particular textured hair, and then ultimately pull it out. If it breaks, it leaves anxiety, so often the quest for finding a similar hair begins. Often, I would not know the extent of the full damage until it was over, due to the pulling occurring while I'm in a trance-like state. My goal, now, is to wait-out the urges, for I have found hours, sometimes days, later the urge to pull has passed. However, getting to that point takes a great deal of work. It's entirely up to your child when she's ready, if ever, to take the necessary steps to make that happen.

To help you understand your child, ask yourself the following question: Do you have any vices you use to relieve stress or anxiety? Try to relate how you'd feel if someone told you to just stop. That's the same way your child feels. Try to let go of thinking this is something for you to control. Instead, be there for her. Be there like you wish someone had been there for you. Remember, one of the best gifts that can come from Trich is the opportunity to develop a closer relationship with your child. Struggles either make us stronger or they tear us apart. So, by accepting your child unconditionally, it will create an opportunity for both of you to grow stronger together.

Provide a safe place and be a safe person. Connect with your child. Address your child by reassuring her of her value and preciousness. Tell her, even if you don't exactly feel it, that it wouldn't matter if she ever stopped pulling her hair, that who she is simply isn't defined by her appearance. Rub her hands, feet, back and head to calm her nervous chemistry, and soon she'll feel a sense of peace.

If you haven't already created a safe relationship with your child where she can come to you, it's never too late to start. The best gift you can offer your child is the truth about who she really is. It is for this reason, I often share age appropriate personal stories with my children. They love to hear about when I was a kid, especially when I was naughty.

No one cares what you know, until they know you care. Let your child know you're there for her in every way you can be. She'll appreciate your trying and be thankful you are not adding additional pressure to her life. Remember, ultimately, Trich is her battle. As your child discovers the emotions behind her pulling, she'll learn how to control the behavior.

Where else can our children learn unconditional love, if not within their own family? How sad when it's not available. Most likely, you have made many mistakes in the past. Just being a parent makes that inevitable. It's a tough job, at best, but fortunately, kids are truly resilient. They want so much to have relationships with their parents, and we, as parents, need to lead them by example. If we don't know how, which we most often don't, then we need to work on ourselves first, before we can offer our kids the help they need.

In order to do this, we need to possess humility. To be able to see our own mistakes and be honest with our children will deepen our relationships with them, as well as anyone else in our lives. I sometimes have to apologize to my children when I get angry, and confess to them that I am not perfect. I knew internally that since I didn't hear that growing up, it's important for me to let my children know I'm not perfect, and that I love them very much. They're aware I'm always trying to better myself and that I care about my relationship with them. It's important to interact with your child in a way that protects and enhances her self-esteem.

We really do live what we learn, and now is the time and opportunity to instill in your child the keys and skills of life you might not have been able to give until now. The fact is, you cannot offer what you don't have, and that's why I say Trich can be a blessing in the lives of everyone involved. Think about it—if it has brought you to a place where you realize you need to change, then you, too, will have benefited as well.

Ask your child what she'd like from you, what you're to do if you see her pulling her hair. Recognize that this is your child's battle. Trying to control her, or make her stop, will simply not work. It will only complicate the emotional ordeal your child's already experiencing. Healing, for the most part, is an inside job. Putting pressure on your child will only bring more shame/embarrassment/frustration and eventually, more pulling into her life.

How your child lives the rest of her life, and the one she chooses for a mate is greatly influenced by how you treat her. Try your best to love your child unconditionally, and if you have trouble doing so, then ask yourself what is blocking your path. Maybe you never learned to love yourself unconditionally. Please let me encourage you by saying that changing a few perspectives will alter the relationship between you and your child, actually bringing you closer through this experience and helping her create a healthier life. Always remember, it's never too late to leave the destructive path you find yourself on and emerge, once and for all, on a journey towards healing.

Quick Tips and Reminders

✦ To better understand your child's hair pulling behavior, look at the ways you handle stress. What behaviors do you engage in that helps you deal with your own inner anxieties.

✦ Remind your child there is a purpose in her having Trich.

✦ Attend a conference together. Go to Trich.org and you will find numerous gatherings that will fill you with a wealth of valuable information and allow your child to discover she is not alone.

♣ CHAPTER 6 ♣

HOW TO HELP
YOUR CHILD

Most likely, your child is critical of herself, so feeling your disappointments will only add to her anxiety. Overall, your child needs your unconditional love and support. She needs you to help her change her perception and see her ultimate value and potential. In this world of mixed up standards, there is incredible stress for our kids to endure. I make it a point to identify with my children, so they know, without a doubt, they're not alone with their feelings, and that they're safe to share them with me. Although you can't force your child to stop pulling, you can provide an environment within your household, and within your relationship, that cultivates a safe zone.

Some of our experiences, of course, will be different from theirs, but most likely our struggles are similar in nature. Help your child identify her behavior and to validate her feelings are normal. Trichotillomania, along with other disorders, causes the most damage from the isolation it creates. I believe with all I have experienced, feeling alone and different caused me more harm than the actual hair loss. When I discovered in my early 30's that I wasn't alone, and that other people felt the same types of inadequacies, I began to emotionally reconnect with others.

As your child learns to identify the reasons for her hair-pulling behavior, her understanding and her value system will change internally. We need to grasp that children often go outside the family for support and love when they don't feel good about themselves or secure in their relationships with their parents. If your child is happy in her life, she won't want to shut down and medicate her emotions. As parents we need to examine ourselves, as well as our households, and make sure we're providing the best environment possible for our children. We're designed to be a protective covering over our kids and to teach them the skills they'll need for the future. Giving your child structured discipline will help her throughout her entire life. Otherwise, where do you think she'll learn how to function in the world?

Nurture your child and teach her to nurture others as well. Do you reach out to others in a compassionate way? Do you volunteer? Do you encourage your child to do so as well? Most of us aren't born with the sensitivity we need to have. So, as parent, we should model a life of maturity, so our kids have a path to follow. Parents need to raise the bar for their children so they reach for higher values. It's our job to teach them to put into perspective situations and emotions and become better individuals in the process.

Be fair with your child. I have to be on guard constantly, especially as I home school my younger kids. I'm quite aware of how my attitudes and moods impact my children. In response, I'm constantly weighing my words and tone. Be watchful and pay attention to your child. This will allow you to get to know her intimately. It will not be lost on her when you show effort to improve your relationship.

Ask your child how you can help. Let her know the answers are up to her, because Trich really is her issue. Let your child know there's help available, but it's her decision when she's ready. Then you need to let go. This is definitely not easy, but there's no other option that's safe. It's far more important that you are there emotionally for your child, then it is to get her to stop pulling. Loving and respecting your child is going to be a major jumpstart in her life.

If you have pressured your child, and all of us have at some time or another, apologize. Let her know you are working on yourself and that you won't be pressuring her anymore. Yes, you will inevitably make more mistakes, (we're only human) but she'll honor your good intentions. Ask your child what she wants you to do, if anything. Does she want you to gently remind her, if you see her pulling? Does she want you to say nothing? Honor her wishes. Always be gentle. Inform yourself, understand your child, and forgive yourself for past mistakes.

People often treat their anxiety with ritualistic behavior, and refraining from pulling may actually increase their anxiety. Try to reduce your child's anxiety the best you can. Look at her situation, circumstances, influences, and pressures and help her to rid herself of as many tensions as possible. If the anxiety can be controlled, reduced, or eliminated then there's a much better probability that your child's compulsion to pull will be reduced to a manageable point. As emotional balance was attained in my life, the need to pull was virtually eliminated. Before we can raise truly healthy kids, we need to be healthy ourselves. When we are anxious, there's no doubt, our children will feel anxiety too.

We need to learn to utilize other coping mechanisms. Taking deep breaths, walking, taking a relaxing bath, etc. helps relieve the pent up stress that's in our hands and throughout our bodies. Over the years, as I've modified my behaviors, and chosen new ways to deal with stress, my life has become less agitated physically, chemically, and emotionally. My crooked lashes no longer captured my attention with such overwhelming interest.

I remember years ago, when I was a manicurist, I had a client named Candy with a background in the Peace Corps. She shared a story with me that I'll never forget. There was a little 5-year-old girl she once took care of.

Yet, due to malnutrition, and lack of stimulation, she responded as a six month old. However, as Candy gave her vitamins and food, she noticed the girl playing peek-a-boo, and soon afterward, the child began tossing a ball back and forth. Then, the little girl started to say the word, "No". Within six months, her development grew from the baby stage to the proper age appropriate behavior. Candy explained, if we don't experience life as we should, and simply shut down, when we turn back on, we'll often pick up where we left off. Life has a process, and if we bypass it, we'll have to go back and redo it.

Children look for limits. A child that does not have rules, who can manipulate and control her parents, is a child who'll be insecure and will have trouble developing self-control. Self control is essential to combat the impulses to pull. As your child matures, discipline will help her internalize control when you are not there. You want your child to learn to say "no" to herself. That's maturity, which so many of us still struggle with as adults. Parents need to teach their children to discipline themselves by providing rules and boundaries, because, ultimately, those boundaries will give them freedom.

I've seen many children who are rebellious and obstinate and threaten to pull their hair, if they don't get their way. Don't let your child manipulate you with such threats. You have to let go and let your child know her choices are her own. I have told my kids many times, their choices have consequences, and whether the consequences are positive or negative depends on the decisions they make. If your child tries to manipulate you with hair pulling threats, inform her that you're there if she wants your help, but that you will not be manipulated. This puts the responsibility in her hands, literally, and helps her realize she has a concrete decision to make. That's an enormous lesson to offer your child. Good choices result in good consequences. Bad choices result in bad consequences. You need to cut the apron strings, so to speak, and let your child know she needs to make the decision to stop. I believe teaching your child to discipline herself as she grow up will help her have an easier time in life over-all.

Always, examine the filter by which you view the world. When you first identify your own issues, you'll be better able to understand your child's pulling behavior. Heal your own issues and your children will follow. As parents we must always take the lead, setting a positive example for our offspring.

If your child knows she has to be nice to others in order to have friends over to play, watch TV, or listen to music, she's more likely to do so. Teach her to get along with her siblings. Don't allow children to hurt each other. Set the bar high. Kids will rise to whatever their parents insist upon, if it is appropriate. We need to teach our children love, forgiveness, sharing, etc. They don't just attain those skills by magic.

So often parents think children simply need to be tended to, watered, fed and clothed. It's just not true. Children need, and want, our instruction and guidance. Children were never meant to be left alone to teach themselves the life skills needed to live a productive and happy life. It's our place to be their guides. Let's make sure we lead them in a positive direction.

Much like alcoholics who stay stuck in their behavior, because they don't work on the emotional issues that provoked them to drink in the first place, many have the same experiences with Trichotillomania, often looking in the wrong direction to try to fix the behavior instead of looking within. Help your child to see inside her soul, to better understand what makes her tick, so she can learn to control her own behaviors as she matures.

In my family, we have rules and standards that my husband and I set which have at times been strict, yet our children have learned to uphold them. Children need structure and rules. Set new standards with your child. Don't allow her to be disrespectful to you, and go a step further by setting a rule for yourself, that you also aren't allowed to be disrespectful to her. Don't lose sight of your role as a parent. Realize that you are to raise your child, and teach her values, until she matures and becomes an adult. Your friendship will be deepened because you were there for her, directing and guiding her all the way.

If you are in a power struggle with your child, then you need to get serious about getting your authority reestablished. There are some wonderful books available to help you to do so. Dr. Phil's, Family First, is filled with valuable ideas. The goal of disciplining your child is for her to internalize your values and then draw from them in a multitude of situations she'll ultimately encounter in life.

Children are looking for limits. I believe every child wants to know there are boundaries and to learn to live inside them. This gives them security knowing they are being protected, and that they know where the lines are clearly drawn. If they know the rules, and the consequences, it will help them make better choices. Having limits will help your child in every aspect of her life, including having positive self-esteem. Learning discipline will teach your child self-control and will help her say no more easily to the things she wants to resist.

Give appropriate lessons, not punishments, unless the situation merits it. Even then give the punishments as consequences, without shaming. Here's an example: My kids' job is to clean the kitchen every night. But sure enough, when I came downstairs this morning, I found they'd left food and dishes out all night and everything was covered with ants. My first inclination was to get angry and clean the kitchen myself. Then I thought it through and decided to have my kids discover the ants on their own, and let them do the cleaning. And what do you know, it took the fume right out of me, realizing I didn't have to let this ruin my morning. Now I know, the kitchen will be taken care of, and at the same time, my kids will learn a valuable life experience. Next time, I bet they'll think of their responsibilities more aptly because they won't want to do double work the next morning.

Remember, every action has a consequence. I believe, as parents, our job is to teach our children life lessons before they are out in the real world. They need to have a safe place to learn with the freedom to fall. Children need our nurturing, just as a little tree needs supports planted on each side. Then, as the tree grows stronger, the supports are brought out further away until it has a healthy trunk, strong enough to withstand the wind and rains. Eventually, the supports are removed all together.

Our children need to learn to take charge of their lives. They need to grasp they teach others how to treat them and that, in many ways, they create their own experiences. Children need to be accountable for their decisions. They need to forgive others, so they won't internalize anger. Without a doubt, there's power in forgiveness. After all, what has anger and resentment ever done for you?

Trichotillomania is like a thermostat, and as your child learns to read her body's reactions, and her behaviors, she'll have more control. When the urge to pull is upon me, I now know to ask myself, "Why do I want to pull right now?" In the beginning, I didn't have the answers, but I knew instinctively there had to be a reason. Over time, I began to realize there was usually a trigger that preceded my desire to pull. Perhaps, I'd just ingested too much sugar or caffeine. Sometimes, I'd just encountered a stressful situation. To better calm myself, I had to understand what triggered my urge to pull in the first place. Without a doubt, awareness is key to healing.

Be patient with yourself and your child. Confide in her, within appropriate guidelines, about your own struggles and that will encourage her to confide in you. Always identify with your child, and, most of all, embrace her heart.

Quick Tips and Reminders

✦ Don't let your child use hair pulling threats to manipulate you.

✦ Teach your child to be accountable for her own actions.

✦ Children need structure and thrive on parental guidance. If you're in a power struggle with your child, don't be afraid to be the parent.

74

Cheryn at 4 months old

Cheryn's 7th and 8th grade pictures before and after pulling began

Jessica (left) 7 years old with sister Alyson (note Jessica's missing eyelashes)

Mikaela at 2 years old holding baby brother, Michael, after pulling of "Bear Bear" began.

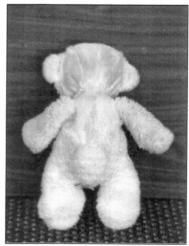

Jessica, Cheryn and granddaughter Madison (2002)

Cheryn's children (top to bottom, left to right)
Jessica, Alyson, Mikaela and Michael (2004)

Cheryn and Mike

♨ CHAPTER 7 ♨

RELATIONSHIPS

When I was young, I had no clue how to have positive relationships. I didn't have one with myself to any degree, so I didn't have anything positive to offer others. That may seem exaggerated, but it's not. I was immature and self-centered. I was also moody and, consequently, spent a great deal of time by myself. It hurt that kids didn't seek me out. If people did ask me over to play, it was usually because their other friends were too busy.

I always admired the popular kids in school and wanted so much to be like them. I tried out for treasurer, pom-pom girl, and school secretary over a three-year span and finally gave up after experiencing failure upon failure. Once, after the meanest girl in the school won the secretary position over me (and mind you, it was a secret ballot, so she didn't win because she threatened people to vote for her) it confirmed my belief that no one really liked me. In addition, the cruel teasing from kids made me feel horribly isolated.

I know first hand the pain that comes when kids tease. However, I now realize as an adult, these kids were simply trying to make themselves feel better by bringing me down. I wish I could have comprehended that back then, because it affected my self-esteem far into my 30's, but that was a difficult concept for me to grasp at the time. As parents, we need to keep reinforcing acceptance and unconditional love to our children. This world has a lot of twisted "values," and we have a great opportunity as our child's parent to teach them the truth about their worth.

One of the concerns teenagers with Trich often share is the fear they'll never marry or have good friends. I've learned, from experience, that we don't need people in our lives that refuse to accept us for who we are. Who needs criticism and judgment heaped upon them anyway? Yet, for reasons I understand now, but didn't then, I drew negative people into my life, for many years. I thought I deserved their ridicule, and it was somewhat comfortable to be around individuals with a negative message, rather than people who were kind and loving. Guys that were nice bored me. Like many others, I looked for drama in the bad boy. Now, as I've matured, I won't allow anyone in my life that doesn't treat me with respect and love.

A real friend, or potential mate, will be one who sees our beauty from within and accepts us without conditions. Appearance doesn't have anything to do with who we really are. Unfortunately, we are told in magazines and movies that success is being thin, rich, and young and that if we are handicapped or old, we are worthless. Translation: "Worth Less."

Many who struggle with self-esteem issues act out their insecurities by jumping from relationship to relationship and/or over-indulging in drinking and eating to fill the void in their souls. I know I did, until I learned to examine my choices and look into my heart to discover the bigger picture.

I believe the best marriages are those where the mate has a maturity where he/she is able to see past the outside package and identify the others value and beauty from within. My husband once told me he feels honored when I take my makeup off in front of him, because I wouldn't do that in front of anyone before him. He saw my inner beauty, even before I did. It didn't matter if I was overweight, had eyelashes, or not. He saw the entire picture, one that I was incapable of seeing for years. I now know there are many people like that, and they enter our lives at the most wonderful, and sometime unexpected, moments.

It's crucial that you speak into your child her value and preciousness, through both your words and actions. If the people who live with her day in and day out, who know her best, think she's incredible, then she'll have a strong, healthy foundation to work from.

Let your child know there are many wonderful people in the world, and that she needs to be selective about who she chooses to associate with. If she learns to accept herself, just as she is, she will draw those into her life that treat her right. If you teach your child to understand why some people are negative, due to their own insecurities, she will gain strength and discretion from your words.

I believe we teach others how to treat us, and if your child has a healthy self-esteem, she will be more inclined to make right choices. It's so important that we carefully select whom we surround ourselves with, as well as know how to be our own best friend. The key for me was when I learned to set boundaries with others. However, I had to get real with myself before I was capable of getting real with anyone else.

Having good relationships with others does really begin in our own hearts. As we discover our true value, we'll be able to peel the onion, layer by layer, until we reach the center. Only then, will we discover who we really are, who we were meant to be. Hopefully, you'll take the time to discover your inner beauty and talents, and recognize your truths, so you can embrace your fullest potential. Having a positive relationship with yourself will change all your relationships, including the one with your child.

Relationships of any kind can be difficult. I learned years ago, when I had problems with my husband, that I needed to look at myself and see if there was something I needed to change. Once I made my primary focus myself, and he made his focus himself, our marriage began to improve.

That concept applies to relationships with out children as well. When my second oldest child, Alyson, came to me as a teenager and expressed, I was "losing" her emotionally because I didn't listen to her and spend enough time with her, I was shocked. Nevertheless, no matter what my intentions were, I didn't relate to her the way she needed. At first I was angry, believing she was being dramatic and just plain wrong. But soon, I realized I needed to see things through her eyes, because if I was just bent on being right, I might lose my daughter. I needed to understand how she was feeling and why she was feeling that way. Once I put on her glasses, it didn't take me long to grasp how she felt. Immediately afterward, our relationship began to improve, and now, five or so years later, we are closer than ever.

I want to help you, first and foremost, to look at your own life, because it might just be that your child is reacting to something you are bringing into your relationship. Maybe not. But you are an important place to begin, because you are the adult and parent. Your covering over your child is a powerful influence. Our facial expressions, and our reactions, can devastate these little people, even when we don't realize we are doing anything wrong. We need to bend down to their level and take a good look at how they see us. This might sound scary, but it really isn't. Seeing things from their perspective will produce wonderful fruit in your family's life.

In order to heal, we must face our fears and insecurities. Address each issue, one after the other. From that point, it's like a domino effect – with each issue falling away, and out of your child's life. Facing our fears may seem impossible, but it's better to deal with what haunts us than to practice avoidance. Undoubtedly, issues will pop up at some point or another, but it's best to face them one by one, and learn why they are there in the first place, instead of later on when all that remains is the unwelcome baggage.

Another question to ask yourself is, "Who is running our home?" We need to make sure that we are parenting our children and that they are not ruling us. We need to constantly teach our children healthy qualities and characteristics, without being controlling. Children do learn what they live, and they learn the most not by what we say, but by what we do. Our kids need to experience lessons gradually, so by the time they leave the house, they'll have made their mistakes while safely under our care. Again, I say gradually and only age-appropriately. If you give your child more than she can handle, it will result in certain failure. Know your child's maturity, capabilities and decision making skills before your allow her to go to the next step.

Before we can truly raise healthy kids with healthy boundaries, we need to be healthy ourselves and have a clear comprehension of our role as parents. It upsets me when I see boys not taught to do housework or to be kind to their siblings. Often in our society, they are allowed to be inappropriately aggressive and are taught that someone else will take care of their needs, just like mom does. What a burden we put on our sons, and their future mate, if we don't teach them to be responsible for themselves. Their self-esteem will suffer without their ever realizing why. My son and daughters were raised to know how to do all the chores involved in running a home by the time they moved out. It amazes and saddens me how many kids are not equipped to be on their own. Sooner or later, they will flounder and struggle when they move out into the real world. What a disservice we are doing to our kids, if we don't set standards that will help them become successful and functioning adults. Children might complain about responsibilities and doing their chores, but eventually, their confidence and self-esteem will be stronger when they know they can take care of themselves. In this world, where there are so many problems kids can get involved in, it's important to view seriously our role in their lives. How and who we are as parents does effect how and who are kids will ultimately become.

I believe if we raise our children with a strong structural foundation of love and respect, they won't want to indulge in unhealthy behaviors. Why would people who love themselves be promiscuous, or seek after drugs/alcohol to medicate their emotions? An emotionally healthy person wants to live life soberly, not be medicated. A loved child won't be looking for inappropriate affection. I'm not saying that a curious child won't experiment in those directions, but if they do, I don't believe they'll stay there for long. If your child feels loved and safe within her family, she will want better from the world, not less.

When I began to ask myself deep questions, sometimes I received the answers immediately, or in some cases, a week or more later. But, no matter what, the answers always came. Sometimes the answers arrived during counseling. Sometimes they came from a friend. Regardless of the messenger, the answers never failed.

I always knew I needed to look deep within my heart to understand the intent. I hope you can do this in your life. Looking inward has changed who I am, meaning, I now know who I am. It has changed my relationship with my husband and my children. As I began to walk this road of discovery, so did my husband, and then of course, we taught our children to do the same. As a parent, you'll be amazed how self-discovery will enrich your life in so many ways.

What a legacy to leave your children and your childrens' children. As you become healed from any dysfunction in your life, you'll break unhealthy behavioral chains in theirs. If you're a smoker, the likelihood your child will smoke is high. If you don't smoke, then she'll be less likely as well. We break patterns for our children, when we break patterns in our own lives first. We have an enormous hold on our children—both negatively and positively. We need to become as healthy as we can— emotionally and physically—so that our children will view a positive and strong role model. Look at your child not as who she should be, but instead, discover who she really is. Help your child ask the right questions that will help her discover deeply her own identify and worth.

From the beginning, I knew I needed to give my children the guidance I hadn't received growing up. My parents were amazing when it came to providing for my material needs, but due to their own issues they had from their own upbringing, they didn't know how to interact with me in the emotional manner I so desperately needed. Consequently, my goal from the beginning, as a mother, was to have a harmonious home filled with love and respect. Since I was a difficult child who needed boundaries and rules, it was from my lacking that I set out to learn how to parent from the time of my first child's birth. I went to child-rearing classes and read many books. I recognized, I had been a spoiled child who lacked discipline and it impacted my decision-making skills. This resulted in making many bad choices throughout my life. I didn't want my kids to make the same mistakes I had.

The only real manuals we get as new parents is the unwritten one our parents gave us, so don't be too hard on yourself, if you are struggling. However, know that you can change and learn to be a better parent. There are many good books available today, unlike in our parents' day, when there were far fewer resources. There is so much help available in libraries, on the Internet, and in bookstores, that it's inexcusable not to reach out for assistance. Don't wait. Do it today – for yourself and for your child.

Quick Tips and Reminders

✦ If you teach your child that she has value, she will never accept anything less from others.

✦ Teach your child responsibility. You will do her a great service as she matures and must make decisions on her own.

✦ Listen to your child, even if her perception of your relationship doesn't match your version of reality.

CHAPTER 8

BEHAVIOR THERAPY TECHNIQUES

When I realized there was a connection between pulling, my emotions and body chemistry, I began to effectively address my urges and learn to modify my behavior. That's not an easy feat since our emotions and nervous system can be intertwined with the relief that pulling sometimes brings. Many are surprised to discover, there is an actual neurological transmission that occurs with the pull of each hair that can calm the nervous system. Therefore, we need to learn how to meet those needs by choosing alternate healthy and non-destructive behaviors.

One common belief is, if you don't look and touch, then you won't pull. This is true to some extent, however accomplishing this is not as easy as some might think, since your child's chemistry may bring about inner conflict. As a parent, you can offer support and encouragement without using the most common approach, which is to attempt to force your child to stop. As you've probably discovered, that method doesn't work. Obviously, if it did, you wouldn't be reading this book.

I'm amazed at how difficult it's been for me to simply avoid bending my arm in an effort to reach my hair or eyelashes. Many times, I have pulled out several lashes, before I've even realized what I've done. So now, in an effort to catch myself before I pull, I try to make myself aware of every simple body movement. Over the years, I'm amazed at how my awareness level has increased, which has enabled me to make more cognitive choices.

A wonderful book that will help you greatly is The Hair Pulling "Habit" and You, How to Solve the Trichotillomania Puzzle by Ruth Goldfinger Golomb and Sherrie Mansfield Vavrichek. It offers detailed help-aids and step-by-step suggestions for diverse situations, regarding what your child can do to bring awareness to her "habits".

Assuming your child has accepted your offer to help, and she is willing to talk with you when her desire to pull is present, this is your opportunity to help her tune in and identify what is really the matter. Sit down with your child and calmly help her discover what is causing her to feel anxious, depressed, or whatever it is she's feeling. The truth does set us free, and if you can help your child identify truth about herself, she will begin to mature and develop emotionally into a self-aware individual. What a great gift to teach your child. By teaching my own children these principles from an early age, it has amazed me how much it's positively impacted their relationships with others, as well as their attitude toward themselves.

When your child has expressed her feelings to you, help her put the situation into perspective. Calm her anxieties by reassuring her that all you ask is she do her best. Remind your child that she is not perfect, no one is, and that her trials are there to teach her patience and empathy, and most importantly to help her grow.

Often, I struggled with negative thoughts, which provoked many of my pulling episodes. I had to learn to retrain those thoughts, often by casting them away and speaking positive affirmations into their place. We need to teach our children to look inside themselves, but not to over-fixate. I believe that is inclined to happen when someone is overly critical and/or a perfectionist. I believe we are made with a self-centered character, and that part of maturing is learning to look outward towards others as well as to be introspective.

We need to train our children, as well as ourselves, to look more outward than inward. Many times, when I've felt down, but then met someone who's suffered much more than I have, my misery was replaced with thanksgiving. I now realize the importance of my focus, and that when I am consumed with myself, I am more inclined to by miserable. I suggest you get your child involved with serving others so she can learn to get outside her problems by helping those less fortunate. Whether it's volunteer work for those in need, or learning to tune into her friends and family's concerns, she will begin to grasp the broader picture. That new focus will redirect her energy into a positive outcome.

There are many people who don't just pull, but also rub their removed hair or lash on their lip or cheek. This behavior can be just as important as pulling. In the book, "The Hair Pulling Habit and You" it suggests "hand and mouth alternatives." One option is to keep your hands busy by playing with fun to touch toys such as a Koosh Ball or Silly Putty. Mouth alternatives may be chewing gum, sucking on hard candy, or nibbling on raw spaghetti. The authors write in their book about how "to train yourself to notice when you are hungry, restless, or otherwise physically uncomfortable, and then to do something constructive to help yourself feel better before you start pulling". This advice is key. Such alternative behavior modification methods help calm the nervous feeling pullers often experience.

Body awareness is an important factor to help pullers control their behavior. Now that I'm aware when my arm bends and my fingers touch my lashes or hair, I'm able to stop the behavior before I pull that first hair and am wrapped up in the cycle. It's always more difficult to stop, when the behavior has already started. As your child builds her awareness of her own body movements, which will come as she learns to pay attention to herself, she will be able to address the things in her life that precede, provoke and aggravate her pulling.

There are ways to make pulling more difficult to accomplish, but it takes a certain level of desire and willingness. I polish my nails when I know I'm in the mood to pull. I've also had artificial nails put on because it makes it much more difficult to tweeze with my fingertips. Wearing gloves or rubber tips during the night or day are a few other ideas that help many individuals. Anything that will slow your child down long enough so she has an extra moment to be aware of what her body is doing will be helpful. These options will give her the opportunity to make a better choice other than pulling.

I hope now you understand why the growth process is a decision your child has to make. As parents we can really only offer love and support to our kids. But don't worry, they will learn from their struggles. After all, haven't we?

When I know I'm overly tired or feeling anxious or troubled, I'll try to initiate relaxation techniques. Often, I'll find myself without pulling impulses once I've removed myself from whatever environment I was in when the temptation was strong. I might go for a walk, or exercise in some manner, listen to soothing music, and/or take a hot bath.

Often when I'm able to relax, my emotions begin to surface, and I'll be able to think more logically. Sometimes a good cry, if needed, seems to help. Lately, now that I feel my emotions are more in order, I'm able to speak my feelings to people, take care of myself emotionally, and have healthy boundaries with others. Being able to live like this has pretty much diminished all the issues that once preceded and provoked my need to pull.

As a parent, it's my desire that my kids possess these coping abilities as well. That's why I express so much thankfulness to everything Trichotillomania has taught me. My entire family is enriched from the lessons we've learned through the trials we've encountered together. When my kids come to me with their troubles, I almost always utter the words, "Let's find the opportunity and purpose in this situation."

Most people I've spoken with, who have Trichotillomania, tend to be perfectionists. I used to think that was a good thing, but now I realize that attitude was choking the life out of me. I felt I had to be perfect, which is impossible and a heavy burden to carry. The tendency of a perfectionist is also to expect perfection from others. It's important to remind your child to be gentle with herself, accepting her process, trusting life to be as it is. She also needs to grant that same grace to others. After all, no one is perfect. Teach your child to take deep breaths and to speak positive affirmations when she is building stress due to perfectionist thoughts.

When I know I'm enduring a stressful situation, have ingested too much caffeine or sugar, or I'm experiencing P.M.S., I prepare myself so I can bring understanding to the pulling impulses that are sure to follow. If I understand this is a temporary situation, it helps me ride out the wave of temptation.

Try to make sure your child gets enough sleep. Insomnia is common among those who struggle with Trich. There are some healthy natural herbs and vitamins to help us rest more deeply. Check with your local health food stores for suggestions. People with Trich often don't reach the deepest level of sleep they should. This often leaves us tired and easily agitated. When I get enough sleep, I notice my need to pull lessens.

The book, *The Hair Pulling Habit and You*, also suggests creating strategies to help the puller with a reward wish list. This helps motivate the will to try other alternatives besides pulling. I know when I have a goal, with an enticing reward, I'm much more able to accomplish what I've set out to do. Below is a rewards and privilege list from the book:

Try small rewards (which you are able to earn at least one a day) such as:

+ Objects: gum, hair ornaments, nail polish, small amounts of money, candy, stickers or a choice of a small prize from a grab bag.
+ A privilege, like special time with mom or dad, five-minute back rub or skip a chore.

Medium rewards (can be earned 4-7 days) such as:

+ Objects: Paperback book, costume jewelry, cosmetics, art supplies, add an item to a collection
+ A privilege like extra use of car (if you are a driver), rent a video, friend over for overnight, ice cream or skating with a friend, or movies.

Large rewards (can be earned in 2-4 weeks) such as:

+ Objects: an article of clothing, small pet, a CD, jewelry, collectible, or money
+ A privilege like no chores for one week, party, haircut, make-over, special outing, or dinner at a fun place.

Often pullers are talented, sensitive and smart. Learning what makes them who and how they are helps equip us to better understand them. By encouraging your child to find and develop her talents, she will be able to have a strong, positive identity, which will carry her through her school years when so many pressures and attitudes surround her. If she's proud of her accomplishment, and knows her strength of character, it will dramatically improve her self-esteem. When I look back and realize how much resilience I had, to try, try again, I now realize how strong I really was all along. Help your child to see her strength. One of the best things you can do for your child is to help her get involved and find interest in her talents and abilities.

Please let me encourage you when I say changing a few perspectives will change the relationship between you and your child. It will actually bring you closer through this experience as well as help your child begin to learn a healthy way of dealing with her emotions and anxieties.

In conclusion, help your child put her "Trich" into perspective, so that she realizes hair pulling is like any other behavior, or addiction, and that she's not alone, because everyone does something to calm their nerves. Pulling is just what her brain is encouraging her to do when she's overtired, anxious, and/or stressed. When your child knows this, it will help ease any anxiety she has developed about feeling different or "weird." Please remember, pulling is often aggravated when the individual dislikes herself. Your love and support and reassurance will do wonders for your child's overall life, not just concerning her Trich behavior. Building a relationship with your child, and teaching her the techniques to overcome the temptation to pull, is a wonderful opportunity to infuse value and self-worth into her soul.

Quick Tips and Reminders

✦ Teach your child to be aware of her body movements before the hair pulling cycle begins

✦ Encourage your child to look outside herself by teaching her to assist others through friendships and volunteering

✦ Try methods of behavior therapy techniques: rewards for not pulling as well as distractions from hair pulling behavior such as handling koosh balls to relieve stress.

CHAPTER 9

FROM MY MAILBAG

Dear Cheryn:

Thank you for writing your book, You're Not Alone: Compulsive Hair Pulling—The Enemy Within. Your insight into what it's like to have Trich helped me immensely. I have a 9-year-old daughter who struggles with Trich and learning how to handle her needs has been difficult.

I want my child to feel she fits in with others at school and do not want to call attention to her hair loss. Lately, my daughter has asked to wear a wig. Should I let her? I'm concerned it might become a crutch, and then she will never stop pulling her hair. What do you think?

A wig, or even false eyelashes and makeup, will allow your child to feel part of her environment. I believe it will also inspire your daughter to let her hair grow back. Few people enjoy wearing wigs or eyelashes, so I don't believe it will become a crutch. When your child is ready to work on not pulling, she will. Until then, for her to feel "normal" will do more for her spirit and self-esteem then you can imagine. Feel comfortable supporting her in any way you can.

Dear Cheryn:

When I was young, my parents punished me for pulling my hair. They ridiculed me constantly, and although I realize now that I'm in my twenty's, they were just trying to help, the emotional scars are still with me. Lately, I've been suffering from mild depression and feelings of worthlessness. I don't know how to lift my self-esteem when I can still hear my parents' voices from my childhood ringing in my ears. What should I do?

To hear your pain breaks my heart. I truly understand your feelings. I suggest you get into a supportive surrounding by going to a good therapist, and by reading books, like the ones I've listed in my Aids for the Journey chapter. Repeat daily affirmations of your precious value and worth. When in your childhood did you begin receiving the message you weren't good enough? You are God's creation. You must remember your value is not conditioned on your outer appearance, but in who you really are on the inside.

Cheryn, my son pulls his hair out all over his head in half-dollar sized portions. I am trying behavior modification, and so far, it seems to be helping. In the meantime, what can I do to hide the spots?

That question is a little more difficult to answer for boys, because most would probably prefer dealing with taunts about pulling their hair, than taunts about wearing makeup. However, there is a cream that would color the spots to better match the hair color so that the patches aren't so obvious. It's called Couvre and can be purchased on the Internet.

Dear Cheryn:

Next week, my seven year old daughter will be taking her school photos. If I apply eyebrow pencil and eyeliner to make her look less unusual, is there a way to put it on so she doesn't look older than she really is? It's important to me that she keeps her innocent little girl quality and is as natural looking as possible. Any suggestions would be appreciated. Thank you.

I remember when my oldest daughter, Jessica, was getting her first pictures taken without her lashes. She was in first grade and too young to be wearing makeup. I applied (very lightly) eyeliner on her upper and lower lids where lashes naturally grow. It helped take away her blank look. In addition, I did the same with the brows, coloring them in ever so lightly. Just remember, less is more and her pictures should have the natural childlike look you're going for.

Dear Cheryn Salazar:

Recently, after years of frustration with my 10 year old daughter's pulling, I shaved her head in hope of breaking the hair pulling habit. My husband thinks what I did was absolutely abusive, and now, my own mother won't even speak to me. I don't know what to do. Honestly, Cheryn, I was only trying to help. Do you also think what I did was wrong?

Although, I understand you meant well, and you should grant yourself grace for your own mistakes, I do believe that anything that causes a child to feel shame is wrong. As a parent, you have an amazing opportunity to be the voice that proclaims your child's incredible worth.

Go to her right now and give her a big hug. Tell her you made a mistake. Let her know, she should never feel ashamed of who she is. I wouldn't be surprised if this is the stepping-stone that will draw you both closer than ever.

Cheryn: My 12 year old daughter goes to private school. We pulled her out of public school a month ago because of the teasing she was experiencing. I thought the new school would be better, but unfortunately, the ridicule has started all over again. What am I supposed to do now? Should I home school her or talk to her teacher? Any suggestions?

Depending on your temperament, teaching your child at home could be either wonderful or make things even worse. I personally began home-schooling over 5 years ago because my husband's work schedule kept him from seeing our kids otherwise. It has drawn us closer as parents, helped the children grow closer to each other, and the lack of pressure has been beneficial for everyone.

If you are unable to home-school your child, then I would speak with her teacher, offering information and resources such as trich.org to educate her about this condition. Then, I'd ask her to handle this subject with sensitivity in her classroom. In addition, it's always good to ask your daughter directly what she's comfortable with you doing.

Cheryn, thank you for your book, *You are Not Alone: Compulsive Hair Pulling – The Enemy Within.* I read it in one sitting, and it has helped me grow so much as a parent of a child with Trich. Lately, my daughter has been threatening to pull out her eyelashes if she doesn't get her way. I'm terrified of not giving into her. How can I remain a firm, loving parent who disciplines her child and yet not contribute to my daughter's hair pulling behavior?

I've heard of this scenario more than a few times. I think it's important for your child to realize this is her battle. Tell her that it's up to her what she ultimately does. I know that is so difficult to understand, but in all actuality, the situation is out of your hands. You will be doing your child such a disservice if you don't remain a firm and loving parent, willing to discipline her with love. Children need to know they can't manipulate their parents. She needs to grasp the reality that her choices all have consequences. Discipline her with love and don't let yourself by manipulated. Remember, you are the parent.

Dear Cheryn:

Fortunately, my daughter has begun to pull her hair less and less lately due to some behavior modification techniques. We count this as such a blessing. Unfortunately, despite her decrease in pulling behavior, I've noticed very little hair returning to her lashes and head. Has she done irreparable damage to the follicles? Will her hair ever come back in its original healthy fullness?

That's hard to say. I know that whether the hair grows back or not is very individual. For the most part, the hair does return. In your child's case, I'd visit her doctor to see what advice he might offer. In the meantime, keep a positive attitude. Time will tell.

Dear Ms. Salazar:

Please help! No matter how many times I hear the experts say it's not my fault, I still feel I have contributed to my child's hair pulling. I've always tried to be a good parent, but I know I'm not perfect. Are you 100% sure, I didn't cause my daughter's problem?

Also, my husband and I believe that God should be able to stop our child from pulling her hair.† People at our church think her behavior is caused by demons. Is that true? We pray for our daughter everyday. What else do you suggest we do to help our little girl?

No, you absolutely did not cause your child to have Trich. And even more importantly, her condition is not caused by demons. Such negative talk can leave emotional and spiritual scars that last a lifetime. Sadly enough, I was old the same thing when I was young. I realize now, such nonsense was far from the truth.

I suggest you keep praying for your daughter as I, too, believe there is power in faithful prayer. Ask that she develop internally a deep sense of self-worth, and come to recognize your genuine love for her. Always, trust there is divine purpose in her trials.

Cheryn, with all the scientific studies today, please tell me there is some kind of medicine my daughter can take that will cure her pulling? What about anti-stress drugs? Do they help? My doctor doesn't seem to know what in the world to recommend.

This is a tough question. Unfortunately, there is no one miracle pill. Some medications help one more than another. There are drugs known to help reduce anxiety, and used along with behavior modification techniques, can help the puller gain more control over her impulses. In many cases, finding the right answer is more or less a guessing game by doctors.

The Trichotillomania Learning Center does have a Scientific Advisory Board engaged in studies to find breakthroughs to better aid those with Trich, attempting to discover the base cause, so we can combat this obstacle together. Direct your doctor to the website trich.org to gain as much information possible regarding this difficult and often perplexing disorder.

Dear Mrs. Salazar:

Please tell me there is hope for my child's future. When I think about the years ahead, I fall into despair. If my daughter can't handle stress as a ten-year-old, what will she do when she's older? Is there really hope?

Yes, there is hope! Trichotillomania is truly such a tiny part of your child's definition. If you put your focus on it, instead of on her, she will be less likely to see her wonderful attributes and talents. Whether or not your child ever overcomes her impulse to pull should not determine whether your child has a bright future.

Many people, who have suffered far worse, have learned to discover depth and richness through the experiences of their trials. Help your child see her true value and worth, rather than focusing on the negativity that Trich can bring. Remember, hair pulling is not who she is, it's just something she does. Be hopeful in your beliefs, and your child will begin to see the light in her own future.

CHAPTER 10

AIDS FOR
THE JOURNEY

How to find a Good Therapist

Don't be too disappointed if you find there are many therapists/doctors who are not familiar with Trichotillomania. Professionals worth their salt will want to learn more about the conditions they are unfamiliar with. Always be skeptical of anyone who throws out answers without first obtaining the proper information. Direct them to T.L.C. to get information, so they can better help your child. Remember, you are in charge and need to interview the professionals that seek to help your child.

More Help Along the Way

Get online at www.trich.org for all sorts of good information. There's a wonderful quarterly newsletter, support groups, as well as online chat for parents and for children. They also offer annual retreats and conferences across the nation.

Email other parents. Have your child email other kids with Trich. Monitor her activity, so you make sure the contact is healthy and influencing her in a positive manner.

Additionally, pets are a great companion. (We all need to feel the unconditional love that a pet gives) and are known to be great stress relievers.

StopPulling.com is a wonderful resource online that offers interactive behavior program. This website is an easy to use, on-line behavioral program designed to help individuals manage their Trichotillomania. StopPulling.com is not therapy and is not intended to replace individual behavior therapy. It is an interactive behavioral program that will help you to identify situations associated with your pulling behavior, and will recommend strategies to help you to change those behaviors. StopPulling.com is intended for people 12 years and older. The program can be used in conjunction with behavior therapy for people who are already in treatment with a therapist who is familiar with treating Trich. StopPulling.com can be a nice complement to therapy, however, if you are currently in therapy, let your therapist know you are considering subscribing to StopPulling.com, so they can integrate the program successfully into your treatment.

StopPulling.com can also be used by people who do not have access to appropriately trained professionals in their area, i.e., someone who knows how to treat Trich. Because so few professionals are trained specifically to treat Trich, it's often difficult to find someone in your area or on your insurance panel. While StopPulling.com is not therapy, it can provide a useful alternative to a self-help book or to treatment with a professional who is not trained in treating Trich.

Date	Amount of Hairs Pulled	Area Pulled (scalp, lashes, brows, body)	What were you doing when pulling started?	Location	Feelings Preceeding Pulling	Urge (0-10)

A Closing Message from Cheryn

I hope and pray that, after reading this book, you are now wearing new glasses and your life has been changed. I hope you feel better equipped to help your child. I know the changes that can happen, and the courage we can teach our children, when we embrace the right attitudes and tools in our own lives. Teach your child to move on with life and not allow trials to hold her back. Life is always so much bigger than we comprehend, as many of us discover on our own inner journey.

Although my prayer used to be, "Please God, stop me from pulling, and while you're at it, help me lose my extra weight." Now it is, "Please, Lord, help me learn absolutely everything I need, so I will discover the truth of who I am, and I can live more authentically." Remember, trials are here to teach us who we are. Once we comprehend what we need to learn, the trial will be over. But don't get too comfortable, there will soon be another lesson on the way.

Embrace the teaching tools that come into your life experience. Don't resist them. They are there for a reason. Then, teach your child to view her trials the same way. If you do, I believe with all my heart, you'll have given your child an essential key to life. Ultimately, it will transform every aspect of her experience, as well as the individuals she's sure to encounter in the future.

Remember, you need to be your child's voice until she can find her own. You are her covering until she's an adult. You were hand picked to be your child's parent. Teach her to look at struggles as an opportunity to grow. Otherwise, our tendency as humans is to withdraw and shut down. It's then that the temptation to become a victim occurs. Instill the truth of your child's value into her heart and mind. Teach your child that she is beautiful, intelligent, and wonderfully made. Even if you don't believe it wholeheartedly about yourself, perhaps due to your own inner dialogue, speak the truth of value into your child's being. Remember, it's not about feelings; it's about truth.

As for my journey? Today I'm pull-free with lashes, brows, and a full head of hair. But even more importantly, I feel free inside myself. I've overcome issues with perfectionism, self-hatred, abandonment and rejection. I've learned to allow myself to really feel and to identify my feelings.

By watching myself grow, and seeing my life changes, my husband and children have also learned to address their own issues. That's why my marriage to Mike is healthy and happy and continues to improve, and why our children are well-adjusted, self-aware individuals who are engaged in healthy relationships. Of course, as long as we are on this earth, there will always be areas in our lives that require growth. No doubt, perfection doesn't exist in my world, but there's definitely a healthy foundation and living skills that are available to anyone who reaches out for a better life.

After all, don't we really want our children, as well as ourselves, to have a happy, functioning and productive life, with the ability to make a positive difference in the world? I certainly want more for my children than I ever had. A brighter future for your child ultimately begins with you, the parent. I promise, if you decide to take this adventure together, you'll be rewarded, not only by a better relationship, but also by the wisdom Trich will bring into your lives.

Let the healing begin.

Suggested Reading, Visual Aids, Products and Other Resources

Books:

You Are Not Alone: Compulsive Hair Pulling

"The Enemy Within"

By Cheryn Salazar
This book is about a woman's struggle with compulsive hair pulling and her recovery process, emotionally and physically, from this devastating disorder. Her sensitive and personal insight into this issue offers hope and inspiration. This book is easy to read for adults or children 10 years and older.
Available through Cheryn.com, Trich.org, and Amazon.com

The Hair Pulling "Habit" and You
By R. Golomb and S. Vavrichek
This workbook for young Trichotillomania sufferers is written in plain common-sense language and allows each user to tailor the program to his or her own needs. The information is highly accessible to children, and is based upon the latest under-standings of Trichotillomania. Recommended to younger people, parents, and therapists as well.
For more information go to www.hairpullinghabit.com
Available through TLC's Book and Video Order Form @ trich.org as well as Amazon.com

The Hair Pulling Problem: A Complete guide to Trichotillomania
By Fred Penzel, Ph.D.

This book includes all the information a patient or relative would need to understand this illness and cope with it. Dr. Penzel provides a detailed discussion of the causes and he reviews all the treatment options, with particular emphasis upon cognitive and behavioral therapies, as well as the most effective medications and their side effects. He shows patients how to design a self-help program and gain control over their compulsive behaviors, how to prevent relapse, describes Trichotillomania and its treatment in children, and suggest coping strategies for families at home and in public situations.

Available through TLC's Book and Video Order Form @Trich.org as well as Amazon.com

Help for Hair Pullers: Understanding and Coping with Trichotillomania
By Nancy J. Keuthen, Ph.D., Dan J. Stein, M.D., and Gary A. Christenson, M.D.

This book reviews the latest treatment options and offers effective cognitive-behavioral techniques for controlling this disorder. For more information go to www.trichhelp.com

Available through TLC's Book and Video Order Form @ Trich.org as well as Amazon.com

Trichotillomania
By Dan J. Stein M.B., Gary Christenson M.D., and
Eric Hollander, M.D. (editors)
This book has been written from a clinical and
a research perspective by psychiatrists,
psychologists, and researchers and covers issues
such as assessment, childhood Trichotillomania,
the role of hypnotherapy and the relationship
between Trichotillomania and OCD. The use
of medication, the place of a psychodynamic
perspective and the value of behavioral
interventions are also thoroughly discussed.
Recommended for treatment providers, and people
studying Trichotillomania.
Available through Amazon.com

*Your Best Life Now, 7 Steps to Living At Your
Full Potential*
By Joel Osteen
A marvelous book about reaching the potential
you were born to embrace. Available at bookstores
nationwide and on Amazon.com

The following books are by Henry Cloud &
John Townsend:
Boundaries
Boundaries with Kids
Boundaries in Marriage
Raising Great Kids
Raising Great Kids for Parents of Preschoolers
Raising Great Kids for Parents of Teenagers
How People Grow
Changes That Heal
Safe People
The Mom Factor
Make Room For Daddy

The Following Books are by Dr. James Dobson:
*Parents' Answer Book: A Comprehensive Resource
From America's Most Respected Parenting Expert*
Preparing for Adolescence
The New Hide or Seek
The New Strong-Willed Child
The New Dare to Discipline
Parenting Isn't for Cowards
Bringing Up Boys
Night Light for Parents
Certain Peace in Uncertain Times
Dr. Dobson: Turning Hearts Toward Home
*Love Must Be Tough: New Hope for Marriages
  in Crisis*
*Complete Marriage and Family Home
  Reference Guide*
Straight Talk to Men

TLC Email News List:
Sign up today! This is a free and easy way for you to stay up to date with TLC and Trichotillomania. When you sign up for this email list, you will receive a message anytime there is news from TLC.

TLC will send you email about:
Scientific research reports
Research studies you can participate in
Conferences, retreats
Local networking events
Media appearances
New resources, books, organizations, and products
TLC Volunteer projects
How you can help TLC

**TRICHOTILLOMANIA
LEARNING CENTER**
207 McPherson Street, Suite H
Santa Cruz, CA 95060
ph: 831.457.1004 • fax: 831.426.4383
www.trich.org

Videos:

"Our Personal Stories – The Truth of Trichotillomania"
TLC has produced a documentary video on the experience of Trichotillomania called "Our Personal Stories – The Truth of Trichotillomania." This video expresses some of the life situations and areas of personal grief and recovery experienced by the eight women on the tape. For anyone seeking personal insight into this disorder, this tape is highly useful.

For more information for purchasing this video go to www.trich.org

"Bad Hair Life" – A documentary film by
Jennifer Raikes
This vivid one-hour documentary explores the often deeply secretive disorder, Trichotillomania, or compulsive hair-pulling. The idea for this film grew out of the personal experience of Jennifer Raikes, a producer at Middlemarch Films, who has had Trichotillomania for over 20 years. Five years in the making, the documentary is the first in depth portrayal of this complex disorder and the profound impact it has on the lives of those struggling with it.

The documentary presents intimate portraits of adults and children at different stages of coping with hair-pulling. Using art, photography and interviews, *Bad Hair Life* examines the importance of hair to our identities and the cultural forces that make this disorder feel shameful.

The director shares her own history with hair-pulling, starting when she was nine and idly pulled out her first eyelash, through years of embarrassment and hiding, to her present quest to understand this mysterious behavior. Expert researchers and clinicians discuss the disorder's causes and treatment. But the film's greatest power is in its intensely honest, first-hand accounts of life with Trichotillomania. For more information for purchasing this video go to www.trich.org

Products Specifically Developed for Those Who've Experienced Hair Loss

Cheryn International is a company that grew out of Cheryn Salazar's personal experience with Trichotillomania. She developed a line of truly natural-looking false eyelashes and various makeup products to subtly enhance the beauty of those who have experienced various types of hair loss. Cheryn's desire is to provide a feeling of normalcy and beauty.

For further information, or to contact Cheryn Salazar, please write or call:

Cheryn Salazar

866.324.0908 • 916.804.1337

CherynS@Cheryn.com

www.Cheryn.com | www.TheWigEmporium.com

9886672R0

Made in the USA
Lexington, KY
06 June 2011